Don't Tell Me It's Okay

Sue Doble

authorHOUSE®

AuthorHouse™
1663 Liberty Drive
Bloomington, IN 47403
www.authorhouse.com
Phone: 1-800-839-8640

First published by AuthorHouse 11/17/2010

ISBN: 978-1-4520-8784-9 (sc)
ISBN: 978-1-4520-8785-6 (hc)
ISBN: 978-1-4520-8786-3 (e)

Library of Congress Control Number: 2010915713

Printed in the United States of America

This book is printed on acid-free paper.

I come to prosper you not to harm you, I come to give you the future that you hoped for (Jeremiah 29:11)

Table of Contents

Foreword

Sue Doble and I have been the best of friends for many years. She is a warm, giving person whose world has been rocked by the death of her husband of forty years.

Sue felt God leading her to write this book, and so she pushed forward in her grief. This task was not easy, yet she persevered, at times with passion and at times numbed by her pain.

She is a godly woman, who reaches out through this book to share of herself and her experience with those who walk this same valley and to forewarn those who watch the struggle through the pain to value what they have now and work out problems in relationships before it is too late. At times throughout this book you will feel her raw grief and pain, so willingly shared. At other times, you will share in her anger and despair. All you feel and hear in the words is from her heart to yours. Sue is begging you to live life as though tomorrow will never come. The only way my friend has been able to withstand This time is through her walk with God. Many times she questioned whether He was listening and despaired He did not hear. Watch and learn from her, because God has given us the best example to follow. I believe my friend is finding strength in God in ways she has never experienced before.

It is my belief that you will find the answers to all circumstances in this life through her ravaged walk. Trust God with all your heart and lean not on your own understanding (Proverbs 3:5). This is where Sue is, and she will take your hand and walk with you to discover the greatest answer to life's struggles through this book.

May God bless you with time to mend what needs mending, especially with the one who matters most—God.

Shelley Mason

Preface

Family Dynamics

I will introduce you to my family, so as you read the pages and the names appear you will then know whom I am talking about.

Our oldest is Goldie, and she is married to Jordi. They have two sweet but typical boys, Parker and Aidan.

Ernie is married to Kim, and they have six children. Their names are Joe, Kurtis, Caleb, Curtis, Kurstyn and Ethan.

Shane is married to Terry, and they have two children, Lacey and Cole. Cole takes after Papa for size.

Jenny has two children, Nathan and Kourtney.

Gordon has four children, Shyanne (whom I am raising), Shilo, Dakota and Julie.

Brendan has a daughter, Kennedy, and is living with Erin.

Shayla is living back home with me, to help me through this time.

Acknowledgements

With Special Thanks

First and foremost I want to give thanks to my Lord and Savior Jesus Christ. If the Father had not carried me through this dark time, I would not be here.

This is dedicated to my special friends, Shelley Mason and Helen Burake. They came beside me and were faithful when they said they would never let me go. They would pull, kicking and hollering, so that I would not stay in the pit of hell that had become my existence for so many months.

Murray and Judy Howarth, Bill and Barb Retzlaff, Dave Brown, who was George's brother of the heart, and his beautiful wife, Rose: thank you, my precious friends.

Shane and Terry: Shane, when your dad put you in charge over me to take care of me, you and Terry took on this role, not only with duty in mind, but also with deep love and commitment. It has touched my life in more ways than I can ever begin to tell you. I love you both dearly.

Shayla, you had to put up with a lot when I was in my darkest hours. I sometimes forgot how bad you were hurting as well. This is such a hard thing to go through. It has made the family dynamics so different. You, Shyanne and I are in a place that is hard to comprehend. I love you, my little black-eyed pea.

Ernie and Kim, you are precious to me for the help and love you have extended. I know it was hard with moving, setting up a new business and grieving all in the same breath. I love you for your care for me and for praying for me when I would call crying.

Jenny, though you could not be here, your phone calls and caring have touched my heart and life more than you know. I love you.

Gordon, you helped in ways that astounded me. My heart was so touched, and I truly felt your love in this. I love you.

Brendan, you showed so much love for me at this time. Because of the distance I understand why you haven't been here much. I know your heart. I love you for this.

To the grandkids who gave of their time and love, may God's blessings be upon you. I love each and every one of you.

Introduction

This is a memoir of Sue Doble, George Doble and their family, from the time of Sue and George's fortieth wedding anniversary to one year after George's death. The writings on the pages will hopefully inspire people to see that losing a loved one is a very hard step in life. Grief is messy beyond description.

George was born in Brooks, Alberta, and spent the first thirty-five years of his life between Scandia and Rainier, Alberta. Sue was born in Carmongay, Alberta. She grew up between Champion, Calgary, and Okotoks, Alberta.

George and Sue met in Blunts' nursing home in Vulcan, Alberta. George's grandparents were residents there, and Sue was a practical nurse. They knew the moment they met each other that they were to be together.

This book deals with the fact that Christians fall short in the body of Christ in taking care of their church families, so there-fore cannot reach out the way that is needed to people at large. It is about the pain of letting go. But mostly it is about having Jesus as your Savior and being assured that all will be okay. Not just George had this assurance but the whole family. This can only happen when we let go and let God.

To let go and let God calls for giving up the pain, the hurt, the anger, the rage, the loneliness and any rights you may think you have—the right to a different future than the one you have right now or the one you were looking to have.

The time is now to get on and see what God has for the lives of each of us, not just getting on but also getting excited about it. And so the new journey begins for Sue and her family.

Chapter One

Lamentations 1: 16
"This is why I weep and my eyes overflow with tears. No one is near to comfort me " (NIV).

My husband, George, and I celebrated forty years of marriage on October 28, 2007. Our children had a celebration for us two weeks earlier.

I wanted George to slow down and take time to enjoy life a little more than he was doing. We were both workaholics. We were always raising kids. We had had kids in our house for thirty-nine of our forty years of marriage. We had fostered fifty-four foster kids. Still, to this day, I am raising a child. Our precious granddaughter was born with many challenges that her parents couldn't handle; therefore we took on the challenge.

I bought George a four-wheeler for our anniversary as a surprise for him. He had wanted one for many years but never felt he could afford one. When George was presented with the four-wheeler all he said was "That will do." That was all he said, but his big, beautiful smile and glowing eyes told the story.

Over the last year George had been really tired. I mentioned now and again that he needed to see the doctor. His reply was "I just need to slow down on the work end some." June of 2007, he was more than a little tired, and his right arm was starting to hurt more than usual. Again I asked him to please go see the doctor. He promised me that as soon as the mowing was done for the season he would go in to the doctor. Our company did mowing and grading for the oil companies in our area. Time was as usual: get it done before the weather changes.

I made an appointment for the 7th of November for him. At this time he told the doctor that he was just tired all the time and his right arm hurt real bad. He could not sleep half the time from the pain.

We attributed this to arthritis. We also took into account the fact that George was a big, strong man. He lifted much heavier things than he should have most of the time.

George had had cholesterol problems, and the doctor needed to see if it had changed. The doctor ordered some blood work and a cholesterol test.

By the following Saturday morning, things did not appear to be good for George. He appeared to be disoriented. I thought he had had a stroke. I took him in to emergency, where they also thought that this was a possibility.

The emergency doctor told us to put him on aspirin and if we felt he was stroking out again to give him more aspirin. The doctor said she would check with our family doctor to determine what tests were ordered. I was more than a little upset with her for sloughing this off so lightly. What if he had a major stroke before she found out what it really was?

On Monday morning, November 18th, we went to see our family doctor. He made light of the situation, saying, "You never told me you lost your mind, George." George just laughed, and the doctor said he thought he should order a CAT scan. When the order was in, we went home. On the way home I called various people to pray that George would get in quickly. Usually the wait was three months. I was totally amazed, for when we got home there was a call to come in early the next morning to have the CAT scan.

The following day, the 19th of November, we went to have the scan done. The technician told us to wait while he talked to the doctor. We waited an hour; then we were told to phone our family doctor for an appointment. I did this right away and got an appointment for 2:00 p.m. the next day.

CHAPTER TWO

Lamentations 2:11

My eyes are blind with tears, my stomach in a knot.

The day was November 20th. This was to be the day that changed our lives forever. When the doctor came into the room at the clinic to see us he said, "I have bad news for you."

My thought was that we were going to have a fair bit of rehabilitation to do. This was not to be, for he looked at George and then me and told us that my precious husband was going to die of a cancerous brain tumor.

The doctor proceeded to tell us that this tumor was way down in the middle of the brain, where it was inoperable. It was very fast growing. He also told George to go home and get things in order, for he only had two to three months left.

George and I had seen God perform many miracles, but as we looked at each other we each knew beyond a shadow of a doubt that this was not going to be one of them.

As I drove home with one hand on the wheel, we sat in silence, holding hands. We each were deep in thought. I was frightened and numb in the same breath.

We arrived home to the farm, and I went to put wood on our outside furnace. George insisted that he do it. He needed time to digest the things that the doctor had said as well as some quiet time with God.

I called our pastor and also our friend Murray, who was an elder at the church. George was also an elder, and they had become close friends. I asked them to come at 7:00 p.m. I then proceeded to call all of our children to come to our home by 7:00 p.m. Our seven children ran from nineteen years of age to forty. I called our friends Helen and Dave to bring our oldest over, as she needed a ride. I would not tell them what they wanted to know until they were all present.

As we all sat down in the front room I pulled a chair up close to George's recliner and held his hand. I then proceeded to tell all who were there that the love of my life was going to die. God had chosen to call him home. This wonderful husband, dad and friend, who was so funny, so precious and such a big presence spiritually, physically and mentally, was to be taken from us in a very short time.

All of our children and their mates were crying. I was sobbing as well. When I finished telling them all I had learned about the diagnosis, our pastor asked George how he felt about what was happening.

George said, "The Lord knows this is not what I want for my life, but who am I to argue with God? I know He will look after Sue."

There was no doubt that the Holy Spirit was present with George, as he had a serene peace around him that only comes from the Father.

Chapter Three

Lamentations 1:20

"I am in torment within, and in my heart I am disturbed" (NIV).

That night after everyone left, I sent out this e-mail:

> It is with great sadness I write this. My darling husband has a large brain tumor deep in the center of both hemispheres of his brain. It is fast growing, and the doctor feels we have a matter of a few months.

The e-mails came pouring in. People were shocked and wanted to let us know that they were praying for us. Even people who were not Christians told me that they were praying for us. I have chosen only a few of these e-mails to share.

I called all of the siblings on both George's and my sides of the families. I also called friends. This is what I told them: "George is dying, and the doctor has told us two to three months at the most. If any of you want to see him, then please come now."

As people came over the next few weeks I invited them to crawl up on the bed with him, if he was in it at the time. I also encouraged all who came that if there was anything between them and George to make it right, because we were not promised a tomorrow. I do not know why I thought of this, but it seemed that I needed to do this.

I could not believe the people that graced our home to see George and tell us they loved us and were praying for us. People I never expected showed up at our door to say goodbye and say what an impact we had made on their lives. There were many family members, including grandchildren, who sought forgiveness for things they had done to upset George. Some grandkids had stolen in the past, had refused to do a job Papa had for them or had done other little things that nearly all kids go through. What a blessing that each child and grandchild had the confidence in their papa's and dad's love and forgiveness to go and make things right with him.

Chapter four

Lamentations 1:12
"Is any suffering like my suffering that was inflicted on me that the LORD brought on me in the day of his fierce anger?" (NIV).

It was the second week of December when I saw a dramatic change in my darling husband. Each day his memory became more fractured, he became more weak and the weight dropped off of him. From the start of December to the 16th, George would lose around thirty pounds.

Our son Ernie was checking on a fairly new procedure using a Gamma Knife in hopes of saving his dad's life. (This is a medical device that emits a highly focused beam of radiation, and it will probably save many cancer patients in the future.) George was admitted to the hospital so we could get an MRI. We were in hospital two days, but he thought we were in a hotel.

Here is one of the e-mails that were sent over the next few weeks. For you see, George only stayed on earth a little over three weeks after the date of the diagnosis.

> Dear Sue,
> I am sorry to hear this. Words just don't seem enough. You are very important people to me .George has my utmost respect. He always showed kindness and love to me. He is a true example of a Christian man. He is a man of Grace.
>
> I do not understand why this has happened, but again,

God has a plan. George is just going to beat s home. We still have to go also.

I know this is not easy for you and the family. I will be praying for all of you. Again, I send my love. Tell George, thank you for being George, and I am grateful for him being in my life.

Love,
Ester

Chapter Five

Lamentations 3:3

He took me by the hand and walked me into pitch-black darkness.

I sent this e-mail to update people:

> Today is a good day. This is the day that the Lord has made; I will rejoice and be glad in it.
>
> Sunday George quit breathing but then started on his own again when I started rubbing his chest and crying. He did not look as if he were going to last the day.
>
> Our pastor, friend Murray and family were called in. We knelt and prayed at the bed, as well as sang songs of praise to the Father.
>
> God was so good. He allowed us more time. George rallied up and even got up and had tea with all of us. Not one person who saw him at death's door expected him to make it through the night. Thanks went up to God.
>
> Even as George looked as if he was not to make the night you had to smile. For even at death's door he could not stop tapping his toe ever so lightly to the music of the Gaithers. [Their musical videos were on every hour of every day since he took ill. George more than a little

loved their music and videos.] There were so many prayers, so many blessings of extra time.

Yesterday, and Monday as well, George could not sit up for more than twenty minutes; nor did he want to eat or drink much. Today he has and still is in the wheelchair, around two hours so far.

Parker, our grandson, has a robot car. Papa plays with this, trying to figure it out. He has been thirsty and hungry. He is so sunken in the face, it breaks all the hearts that see him.

Ernie is still checking on the Gamma Knife as there is nothing else that can be done but to make him comfortable. I have increased the steroids and decreased the morphine so that he has some better times with people. He is not in pain at the present time. He is also taking pills for seizures.

Our darling son Ernie has a hard time letting his dad go. We all do, but he is still hanging tight and not releasing his dad. He is the last to do so.

Today George wanted his cell phone. Brendon asked, "What do you want that for, Dad?" George said, "So I can call that hot redheaded chick." What a precious moment for me! This is a forever memory to store up in my heart's memory box.

We will know tomorrow about the Gamma Knife. I will let you know. It is down east, and time would be of the essence. Only the heavenly Father knows. Today is a day of rejoicing. Please pray for our four boys. Today is the day they start to build their dad's coffin. This is what George wanted, and the boys are doing this tough, tough job to honor their dad.

I am so proud of them. The boy's names are Ernie, Shane, Brendan and Gordon.

More e-mails came in:

Uncle George,
I am very sorry to hear this news. It has taken me a couple of days to respond because I have had to process what is happening. It was a shock and brought many thoughts and emotions to the forefront for me. My thoughts and best wishes are with you and the rest of the family.

Hearing this news brought back a flood of memories, like the summers at the farm, learning to care for the animals and the land. I can still smell the grease in the old garage in Rainier, the family assembly line, cutting and cleaning the chickens. Learning how the incubator works and watching chicks hatch. There is nothing like the taste of "real" milk. Then there was the irrigation channel where Gordon used to take us to swim (only now do I realize the danger of swimming there).

I remember the feeling of a familiar but different house and a different set of rules than I was used to. Above all I remember the love I got from Uncle George and Auntie Sue. I remember being so impressed and even intimidated by the size and presence that Uncle George had when he entered a room. I remember the feelings of being safe and well looked after.

I remember being picked up at the airport after our first flight ever. I remember Mom's car spinning into the ditch on our way home from Woking.

I remember the huge lessons in problem-solving and hard work. Because of my experiences on the Doble farm, the Bastian farm and the Burkofsky farm, I have developed a deep appreciation for agriculture and farm life. I have developed great respect for those that dedicate themselves to working the land. I better understand how the will of nature influences life, and I believe that there is a peace and fulfillment that comes with the lifestyle that no city kid could ever understand without the opportunities and experiences that I was afforded with you.

I cannot express how sorry I am to hear this news about your health. It makes my heart shudder and my eyes fill with tears. But above all it makes me feel very lucky, proud, and reminds me just how much I love you and respect you, Uncle George. You are a wonderful man and a spectacular soul. You have the heart of a lion and the determination of that old workhorse from the book *Animal Farm*. You have contributed amazing lessons to my life and have truly helped to shape the man I have become. In my mind and heart you will always remain an example of strength, faith, determination, sensitivity and kindness. You are forever my "Uncle George," a man who fills me with warm feelings and deep respect. You will always and forever be a man who makes me proud and exemplifies strong character. You will always be a man who helped turn an allergic, asthmatic city boy into a caring, hard-working man of balance. I love you, Uncle George. I love you, Aunt Susan. I am sending you every ounce of hope, goodness and prayer I have.

I feel like I have not even begun to describe the affection and appreciation I have for you both. Thank you for everything you have ever done for me, my brother and my mother. Thank you for always caring so much, and thank you for always letting me know that you cared.

May the beautiful music play forever. May we never stop caring and living to our fullest potential.

May this letter bring a smile to your face and let you

know definitely that you are loved and cherished by me.
Your city boy nephew,
Brent

Dear Sue,
I write this with a broken heart to hear of George's diagnosis. Our prayers and thoughts are with you and all your family. We so love you both and covet your friendship. We will always thank the Lord for your time with us in Florida and our time in Canada. Love,
Bob and Bonnie

I sent out another e-mail:

Here is how it goes today. George is too weak to walk, so we are using a wheelchair or bed. He is awake most of the day today and says he has no pain. Gordon stayed at home today so I could have someone to help lift.

The health nurse is out daily to help bathe George. The people at the cancer center for the Gamma Knife need more pictures of the brain. These have been sent, and we will have to wait a day or two.

I look at myself and go, "O ye of little faith." My three-year-old grandson, Ethan, prayed for Papa's healing. When asked to pray again he said, "No, Daddy, I asked Jesus to heal Papa, and so He is healing him." Oh that we should come as a child and have the faith and belief.

George has eaten and drank well today. Each day we have people come whose lives have been touched by this gentle giant. So today is a beautiful day as we rest in the Lord.

Please continue to pray, and may God pour out His blessings on you as you do this for us.

There were more incoming e-mails:

> Hi,
> We know you are hurting and feel your pain. Know that we are with all of you.
>
> Kurtis and Jackie are having supper with me tomorrow night so we can discuss how it will work to close the office for a couple of days and come up. I was going to come up myself, but I know that Kurtis really needs to see the two of you.
>
> My boys are having an extremely hard time with this. Between Christmas and New Year's, I am thinking. I then have to think about flying Brent and Christina to Grande Prairie the same time. I have to have Brent come, and he really wants Christina with him.
>
> Know I am working on things as fast as I can. We love you all.
>
> Your sister,
> Dixie

> Prayer chain is going across Canada and parts of U.S. George and you are being covered in prayer.
>
> Take heart! God is in control, and He is faithful! We have to trust that He knows what He is doing, as hard as this is to comprehend. We are hurting for you.
>
> Love,
> Shirley

> I wish I could be there for you and George in this time of great suffering and sorrow. Know that I love you both and pray for your family. Know that this is such

a painful time, and I am glad you have God to give you strength.

If there is anything you need or any way I can help, please do not hesitate to ask. I hurt for both of you and hurt knowing the man who has been one of my favorite brothers–in-law has to pass in such a slow, painful way.

You are in my thoughts and prayers always, and I will be there if you need a shoulder to cry on as you have been there for me.

Remember that God gives us no more than we can handle to test our faith.

Your sister,
Wendy

Chapter six

Lamentations 2:18

Let the tears roll like a river, day and night.

Paul, my sister Irene's husband, came to bring me coal for the fireplace and see what he could do for us. The tears so easily fell as he came in the door. We held each other and cried. Why? Because he was losing a man that he loved like a brother. Both married into the family yet were like true brothers. Paul offered his help wherever I needed it. What a blessing this was, to have someone come 700 miles to extend love and a helping hand!

Our son Brendan came to help lift his dad, as it was getting too hard for me to do this on my own. Our daughter Shayla gave up her new job in broadcasting to stay at home also and take care of her dad. Both of these grown adult children of ours showed such tender love for their dad with taking a hand in George's care. This is such a hard job, to watch your precious dad deteriorate and die before your very eyes. I could not have asked for better support from our children at this time.

All of the boys—Ernie, Shane, Brendan and Gordon— were keeping equipment fixed for the company, stoves going and any other job that came up. I was not forced to deal with issues that I otherwise would have had to. Our two beautiful daughters-in-law, Terry and Kim, also were blessings beyond measure, taking care of the food, house and errands. Words could never express my love and respect for them.

We tried to keep the tears away from George; he had such strength in spirit at this terrible time in life. We, his family, did not want to let him see the anguish we were in. There was anger with this anguish as well.

Shayla and I each found ourselves hiding in the porch, crouched down by the dryer, so that George wouldn't see us when we could stand it no more and were crying uncontrollably. We had questions it appeared there were no answers to. What we wanted was for George to be content in his going Home and know that while we continue on earth we will be okay.

Did we believe this? Not on your life. How could anything ever be okay again without George here with us?

Chapter seven

Lamentations 3:37
Doesn't the High God speak everything, good things and hard things alike, into being?

Incoming E-Mails

Dear Uncle George,
Wow. What do you say to a person who you know is going to die? I am pretty shaken up from this news. I am sure that other family and friends are too from hearing this.

I am so happy to have seen you in August, even though it was right after Mexico. It is a good thing that you and Auntie Sue came out to see our family. I am sure that this was appreciated even more. It is great that you could come and have a wiener roast, with Shyanne wearing that toilet paper hat. Those were good times.

I am so pleased that you know Jesus as your personal Savior, and you know where you are going when it is time for Jesus to take you home. I am just hoping and praying that others would know Jesus as their personal Savior. That would be awesome.

Anyways I just wanted to let you know you will always

be the person who sold me a pig that I saved a hundred pennies for. I loved that pig and his name Perfect the Pig. I still think to this day it was funny how you said my Shelia doll was ugly. It is very cute looking back.

Unfortunately I do not have very many adult memories. It is hard to see you much when you live so far away. You will always be in my heart, and I am praying that Jesus will take you soon so you won't suffer too much and that Auntie Sue will be able to cope with what comes her way.

I am hoping the family is helping you as much as possible.

I am going to miss you, but the good thing is, I will see you in heaven. I am not going to say good-bye. I will see you later.

Love,
Julie

I had trouble with my e-mail, so the letters did not go out as often as they should have. The phone never quit ringing or the people coming in.

Chapter eight

Lamentations 3:7

He shuts me in so I'll never get out, manacles my hands, shackles my feet. Even when I cry out and plead for help, he locks up my prayers and throws away the key.

Outgoing E-Mail

It is hard to even sit down to write and tell you what is happening. The pain in my heart is so great that I feel it will rip out of me. On the whole George will have about one hour a day where he can function by being up. He has lost over thirty pounds in three weeks. He knows all who visit but has a very confusing time to make conversation. He had an hour two days ago that he spent playing and loving Shyanne. Her little heart is aching as she tries so much to kiss Daddy better.

Shayla has been my rock, helping in the care of her dad and Shyanne. The servant she has been for the Lord and honoring her dad in his care is so beautiful. The older kids have been a godsend. I could not go through this without their love and support. It is so hard for us to see on a daily basis this mountain of a man like a tiny child. He cannot think for himself and has trouble with bodily functions.

We have been blessed that most of the grandkids have been brought to our home and had their pictures taken with Papa. We encourage all who want to see him to come soon so they can say good-bye.

It is so hard to see the Glory of God through this, but I know that this is so.

We have had so many phone calls and e-mails saying what an impact George has had on their lives. We are blessed. I need prayer to continue in my walk with God and to honor my husband in taking care of him at home until the Lord calls him home.

I am selfish and want the Lord to heal him here on earth, but I also want to submit to God for His will, not mine.

Please share this with others who know George, and please continue in prayer.

Incoming E-Mail

Dear Auntie Sue and Uncle George,
Sorry I have not written earlier. It has taken me several days to put together words. I have such a heavy heart praying for both of you and your family. In a time like this it is difficult to know God's plan in all this, yet we continue to pray for His providence.

I have many good and warm memories of Uncle George. I have always found encouragement with my guitar playing from Uncle George. I know he always enjoyed music, and it was nice to have an uncle that was so positive of me pursuing music as a form of worship and enjoyment.

Another memory and trait that I've always been

impressed with is the positive outlook that Uncle George had. I find it encouraging how when we had a chance to visit, he was always looking at the positives and managing to have the faith that the Lord would be faithful.

I thank the both of you for showing your love to me. I have always known that you wanted only the best for me and encouraged me to do well in all I do.

I have always been impressed with how hard Uncle George worked; he had determination that would break a lesser man. Only as an adult can I understand why when you visited you wanted to help with the farm work at Okotoks. What dedication and passion you have shown.

I am reminded of this verse as something you did so well: "*We work hard with our own hands. When we are cursed, we bless; when we are persecuted, we endure it*" (1 Corinthians 4:12 [NIV]). Only a man that is blessed by the Lord can live a life that can be defined by that Scripture.

As I struggle to find words that fit the emotions that I have, I want both of you to know that you have meant a lot to me. I am so glad that you both got to meet Carrie, as she has been such an answer to prayers in my life.

May you both rest in the Lord's arms in this time of tribulation. Our prayers will be there to help lift you up.

With love,
Steve and Carrie

May this verse uplift you like it did for me today: "*Be strong and of good courage, do not fear nor be afraid of them; for the LORD your God, He is the One who goes with you. He will not leave you nor forsake you*" (Deuteronomy 31:6 [NKJV]).

CHAPTER NINE

Lamentations 5:15

All the joy is gone from our hearts. Our dances have turned into dirges.

I sent this e-mail on December 15th near midnight:

> I have not written in a few days as things have been so busy. To be honest I cannot remember when I wrote or what I wrote.
>
> We have had a nurse come and help me bathe George. He has become incontinent in the last two days. We had all the family in this afternoon. George was able to get up and have Chinese food, one of his favorites. My jewel is that George prayed for the family meal. He is so weak it was a whisper, but his love of his Lord never ceases.
>
> This evening we had Murray come over and pray with George. While Murray was here George took a real turn for the worse. Today I have had to administer more morphine than I have ever before. It is nearly midnight and he is still in so much pain, and his breathing is labored. Shane is staying with us tonight. Brendan went home and is so tormented because of his dad. He has not left his dad's side this week, lifting him, changing his bed and pants.

The boys have nearly finished the casket. They say it is beautiful and they are so honored to do this for their dad. They spent many hours on this, but spent them with many thoughts of the past and joy. God is so good, even as we sit here tonight taking turns holding hands with this wonderful warrior of the Lord's and watching the suffering he is going through this night. Even as I write this you cannot deny that God is in control.

As we pray over this wonderful giant the peace that passes all understanding has come over not only my sweetheart but over the family also. We do not know what tomorrow or even the rest of the night will bring, but we do know that the Father is holding us tight.

What an honor to be a servant to my husband, who worked so hard and took care of us all these years. Even as I want to scream *"No, Lord,"* I must submit to this.

Incoming E-Mail

Sue,
Leona and I pray for you every day. We know you are going through, and will continue to go through, some very tough times. We just cannot imagine what the pain is like, and we will not pretend to do so. One of us will someday be facing a similar situation as you are now. All we can do is ask God for the strength to see us through. We know that God's road is straight and narrow and it is impossible for us to understand why He zags when we tend to zig. I believe He is testing your faith and preparing you for a much greater work...His work. We can take comfort in the fact that God chooses to take us home on His schedule, not ours. We know home is that place, heaven, where we all want to be someday.

I have a very special place in my heart for George. He

was one of the few people in my life that had a major impact on my spiritual journey. Although we did not see much of one another, the one thing that stuck with me was what he said: "When you accept Jesus Christ, the Holy Spirit will start working in you, and that is the most wonderful thing of all." Seeing George as a true believer helped me to accept Jesus Christ as my Lord and Savior.

I thank George for his very important part in my journey.
Gilbert and Leona

Hi Sue,
Thank you for your honesty about your feelings. I cannot imagine what it would be like to go through what you are going through. It would be easy for me to sit here in the comfort of "all is well" and say to you "Do not speak words of doubt or despair." But I will not do that. God knows your heart and your pain. I am sure you can tell Him how you feel.

I am encouraged by what you said. "It is so hard right now for me to see the Glory of God through this but I know that this is so." Keep your eyes fixed on Him, because He who began a good work in you will complete it!

We are only pilgrims on this earth. This place is not our home. It is vile and sinful. Our home is with Jesus, where there is everlasting peace, joy and love that is as "ordinary" as air. No more pain, no more sickness, no more tears.

While we remain there is pain, heartache when our loved ones suffer.

Ironically, that pain is a measure of our love for them.

> We still pray for a miracle for George. He has touched our lives as well.
>
> The second stanza of "Sitting at the Feet of Jesus" ends with a tremendous promise: "While I from His fullness gather grace and comfort every day."
>
> Sitting at the feet of Jesus, Where can mortal be more blest? There I lay my sins and sorrows And, when weary, find sweet rest.
>
> Sitting at the feet of Jesus, There I love to weep and pray, While I from His fullness gather Grace and comfort every day.
>
> God bless you and keep you in His care. Daren and Rhonda

This is the song George wanted at his memorial, as it was one he sang often, and he could hardly wait to be sitting there, at his Lord's feet.

CHAPTER TEN

Lamentations 5:17

Because of all this we're heartsick; we can't see through the tears.

GEORGE'S FINAL JOURNEY HOME

It was so hard to get through the days. I had such a hard time accepting the situation even though I knew it was real. I continued in prayer for George. He said he was losing his vision. He thought he had a piece of wood in his right eye. My prayer was something like this: "God, you know how frightened George has always been about ever losing his eyesight. Please do not let him lose his eyesight."

The following day George wanted to do our morning Bible study. He said he didn't need his glasses. Shayla checked to see if he was reading it correctly. He was.

That evening I was praying and asked God, "Please don't let George die in our bed. How would I ever be able to sleep in there again?"

Once again God honored my prayer. That Friday evening George got very restless in bed and had trouble breathing. I had to call Brendon to help me move him into his Lazy Boy chair in the front room. Brendon then let me have some sleep as he watched over his dad. The following morning I said to George, "Honey, I am praying God gives you a clear mind to talk to Ernie."

He asked me what about. I said, "Ernie can't let you go." He said, "Okay."

Around 11 that morning Ernie came and went in to see his dad.

Ernie asked George, "How are you doing, Dad?" George said, "I'm okay, son."

Ernie said, "No, Dad, in here." Then he touched George's heart.

His dad said, "I'm okay, son, but how about you?" Ernie started to cry and said, "I'm not doing good, Dad, not good at all."

George took Ernie by the elbow and said, "Son, I want you to let this go, right now." With that Ernie released his dad. Another prayer answered. This was the morning of Dec 15th, less than fifteen hours before he died.

As the day wore on and the pain started I again cried out to God. "Please don't let George die in his chair. He has had it for so many years."

The health nurse called and told us to send someone to the hospital to get their Easy Boy chair, as it could go into a standing position. Shane went in to Spirit River to get it.

The next morning, December 16, 2007, at 2:45 my beloved passed away. Our beautiful tower of strength went home to His Lord. Shayla and I kissed him and stroked his head gently. I said, "Go home to Jesus, honey; its okay." Shane picked up the guitar and started to sing "Amazing Grace," then stopped to hold his dad's hand as his dad met Jesus face to face.

More than anything, I want to impress on people who know Jesus as their personal Savior and their dying loved one does as well, that they as a family must give permission to the dying person to go home to the Lord. Two days before all of the family had given permission; the doctor thought George had another three months. Did we want to give permission? No! I wanted to grab him by the collar and scream at him, "Don't you leave me! Don't you dare."

Outgoing E-Mails

> On Saturday, December 15, all the family came to have a Chinese dinner with us. It was getting to the point that solid foods were a problem to swallow. George rallied to come to the table and also give the blessings on the family and the food.

At 7 that evening he started to have pain. I had to administer morphine to him at various times between then and around 11:00 p.m. He then slept, though there was pain, till 2:45 a.m.

His breathing became labored. I had asked God to not let him go without me being able to hold him for his journey home to heaven.

Both Shane and I woke, and Shayla was called. We were blessed as we held him as he went home to his Lord and Savior. What a blessing that we could be with him and tell him it was okay for him to go.

My precious children then helped me dress him and get him prepared for his beautiful casket that his sons so lovingly made their dad. Then his sons, grandson and other loving men laid him in it.

Family and friends came to the farm to say good-bye. George was then loaded into his truck he so dearly loved and was taken to be cremated. There, with a felt pen, the youngest to the oldest wrote on his casket their farewells and their promises to this wonderful mountain of a man.

George was my best friend, my lover, my confidant, my helpmate, my strength and my spiritual leader. Till his last breath he could not stop kissing me, hugging me and telling me "I love you honey" and yes, even giving my butt a pat.

I had not been in George's truck since he took sick. The road to Grande Prairie was the longest we have ever known as a family.

I do know that my Redeemer lives, my husband is Home,

and if we keep our eyes on Jesus, we as a family will be okay and will one day be with him again in Glory.

Today being Monday we shall be making arrangements for the celebration of his life. We as a family thank you, for your wonderful love and support of this man, who was and still is so dearly loved.

To let you know that we are having a memorial service for our beloved husband, father and papa, George Ernest Doble. This will be Saturday, December 22, at 11:00 a.m. in Spirit River, at the Centennial Hall. There will be lunch to follow.

Outgoing E-Mail

It seems I am always asking for prayer. Yesterday, Wednesday, Shane's father-in-law died in his arms. His children have lost two grandpas in four days, and Shane and Terry two fathers. Shane was with both fathers and held both as they died. Also, he helped to dress them.

Goldie just got home from the funeral of Jodi's grandmother, who died the same day as George. Also, my friend Helen's mom died the same day as George. She was with me at the time.

George's memorial is Saturday and Wolf's graveside service on Sunday in Manning. Please pray for strength for our families to go the mile at this time. Our most precious friends came to be by my side and show their love and support. I could not go without mentioning them, as they have touched our lives so greatly. These are precious people to me.

CHAPTER ELEVEN

Lamentations 4:17

We watched and watched, wore our eyes out looking for help. And nothing. We mounted our lookouts and looked for the help that never showed up.

I do not remember much about the memorial service. There were so many people and so much love. More than anything, there was so much pain.

This is what was read on my behalf:

> When we first found out about George I read a title of a book, *Embrace the Struggles*. Where there are struggles, there is life. I also know that where there is life, there are struggles.
>
> One of the greatest gifts my precious George was given was transparency. He was the same man behind closed doors as he was in public.
>
> He once told me that the hardest thing in life he had to do when he first became a Christian was to love his Lord and Savior more than me. I never had a problem with this, for as he loved God more his love for me became so much deeper and sweeter.
>
> He was a stern man with his kids at different times in

their lives, because he knew each of them had the ability to succeed in life and become fruitful people in society.

His message to his family as always is "Have you walked the walk with Jesus that is required of you that your walk would be a witness to save even one soul?"

George was always concerned that someone might not have heard the truth of the gospel through him and that someone may have missed salvation through his neglect. This always lay heavy on his heart, and we talked often of this.

About four months ago George came home late from an elders meeting. He said it went well, he really felt the presence of the Lord there, and we would talk in the morning.

In the morning George got up and made me coffee. When I sat down he had a big bowl of water and a towel. He told me he was going to wash my feet. He also said he had challenged the other men to do this as well.

I asked, "Why?" He said to be a true servant of God and humble ourselves before God we first must become as Christ. Christ washed His disciples' feet. This was so humbling and touching for me, I spent the time crying. This memory of his great faithfulness is stored in my memory box forever. I know that as George reached heaven's doors, God said to him, "Well done, my good and faithful servant. Welcome home."

George's favorite color was turquoise, also earth tones. His favorite foods were lemon pie and peach upside-down cake. Even at midnight the first couple of years we were married George would say, "Honey," in a certain tone, and I would say, "I know...'make me a peach upside-down cake, please.'" So many times in the wee hours of the morning we would be sitting there eating peach upside-down cake. In the last few years of her dad's life Goldie would make him this old-time favorite. Not just to butter him up (this did help, though), but to show her dad her love for him.

One of the things he loved most in life was sitting and visiting with people. He loved his farm and thanked God often for it.

He was thankful to have met so many wonderful men when he started the company and did mowing and grading for the oil companies. He prayed for these men and their safety on the job.

George said that when he died he wanted to be known as a man who loved his Lord and his family and did his best. When asked what he loved most about each of his children, this is what he said:

Goldie: Her happy-go-lucky spirit, being a home wife and mom
Ernie: His mind and his mechanical abilities
Shane: His joking and his willing hands
Jenny: Her gentle spirit and her artistic mind
Brendon: His wit and his hands-on knowledge
Gordon: His energy and his love of hunting
Shayla, Her love of the Lord and her singing
Shyanne: Her vim and vigor and her love for all
My wife, Sue: her abundant love and her home abilities

To his daughters-in-law he had this advice: "Always build a life with your husband you can be proud of, and I love you as my daughters."

To his son-in-law, Jordi: "Get with God and be a godly leader. Take good care of my girl. Be kind and loving at all times."

To his friends: "I love you all and have cherished your friendship. Be happy."

Shane wrote a song for his dad and had the opportunity to sing it to George before he died. When he was singing the song he started to cry and was saying, "Sorry."

George just smiled at him and said, "It's okay, son; it's okay." Shane also sang this song at the memorial.

Don't Cry for Me
Don't cry for me Don't cry for me I can't wait for that day
A better place I will be
So don't cry for me

When I heard the news It didn't bother me
Cause in my heart I know God will watch my family Don't cry for me
To my wife of forty years Please don't have no tears
I will look down from above And send down my love Don't cry for me
To my kids I love
With a heart sincere
I'm going to a better place
So please do not fear Don't cry for me
So don't weep for me Don't shed a tear
I'll be waiting for you When you come up here Don't cry for me
The tears fill this page As I write this song
It pains my heart so much Just to say so long
I'll cry for you
I'll see you again Way up in the skies
I'll just remember God's love in your eyes
I'll cry for you
I'll cry for you

George wanted this Scripture read. He wanted it read from *The Message*, for he said even little kids can understand it.

> *There was a man of the Pharisee sect, Nicodemus, a prominent leader among the Jews. Late one night he visited Jesus and said, "Rabbi, we all know you're a teacher straight from God. No one could do all the God-pointing, God-revealing acts you do if God weren't in on it." Jesus said, "You're absolutely right. Take it from me: Unless a person is born from above, it's not possible to see what I'm pointing to—to God's kingdom." "How can anyone," said Nicodemus, "be born who has already been born and grown up? You can't re-enter your mother's womb and be born again. What are you saying with this 'born-from-above' talk?" Jesus said, "You're not listening. Let me say it again. Unless a person submits to this original creation—the 'wind-hovering-over-the-water' creation, the invisible moving the visible, a baptism into a new life—it's not possible to enter God's kingdom. When you look at a baby, it's just that: a body you can look at and touch. But the person who takes shape*

within is formed by something you can't see and touch—the Spirit—and becomes a living spirit. So don't be so surprised when I tell you that you have to be 'born from above'—out of this world, so to speak. You know well enough how the wind blows this way and that. You hear it rustling through the trees, but you have no idea where it comes from or where it's headed next. That's the way it is with everyone 'born from above' by the wind of God, the Spirit of God." Nicodemus asked, "What do you mean by this? How does this happen?" Jesus said, "You're a respected teacher of Israel and you don't know these basics? Listen carefully. I'm speaking sober truth to you. I speak only of what I know by experience; I give witness only to what I have seen with my own eyes. There is nothing secondhand here, no hearsay. Yet instead of facing the evidence and accepting it, you procrastinate with questions. If I tell you things that are plain as the hand before your face and you don't believe me, what use is there in telling you of things you can't see, the things of God? No one has ever gone up into the presence of God except the One who came down from that Presence, the Son of Man. In the same way that Moses lifted the serpent in the desert so people could have something to see and then believe, it is necessary for the Son of Man to be lifted up—and everyone who looks up to him, trusting and expectant, will gain a real life, eternal life. This is how much God loved the world: He gave his Son, his one and only Son. And this is why: so that no one need be destroyed; by believing in him, anyone can have a whole and lasting life. God didn't go to all the trouble of sending his Son merely to point an accusing finger, telling the world how bad it was. He came to help, to put the world right again. Anyone who trusts in him is acquitted; anyone who refuses to trust him has long since been under the death sentence without knowing it. And why? Because of that person's failure to believe in the one-of-a-kind Son of God when introduced to him. This is the crisis we're in: God-light streamed into the world, but men and women everywhere ran for the darkness. They went for the darkness because

> *they were not really interested in pleasing God. Everyone who makes a practice of doing evil, addicted to denial and illusion, hates God-light and won't come near it, fearing a painful exposure. But anyone working and living in truth and reality welcomes God-light so the work can be seen for the God-work it is*" (John 3:1-21).

Our pastor called attention to the need of a Savior, our Lord Jesus Christ. This is what George and I chose for our lives. Because of this I know that he is with the Lord.

As I mentioned in the beginning, we had just celebrated out fortieth anniversary. It had seemed that our whole life was full of more struggles than most people's. We hardly had a breath taken after a struggle before another one came our way.

We felt that if we had not been foster parents for so long, we would not have had half of the heartaches. The other side of the coin was that we would not have had half of the blessings. Many of our children and grandchildren are products of this. We adopted two of our foster children and one child of a foster child and kept another one without adoption.

Three grandchildren came from a second marriage for our oldest son. George and I so easily loved these children, as if they were from our own flesh.

When one of our granddaughters was born with Trisomy 13 syndrome, we had one son and his children living with us and also our youngest child. Our granddaughter's parents moved in with us as well. This made two babies for them. Our household was always busy.

George and I had been praying for quite some time for time for just us. We wanted to travel and started to take time to do exactly that. At Christmastime of 2006 we went with the two youngest girls that were at home to Florida to visit Disney World. In March of 2007 George and I went back to Florida to visit friends.

We had made plans to go to Newfoundland in May of 2008. This was not to be.

A little note I wrote:

> Tonight is New Year's Eve. Shayla is gone and Shyanne is in bed asleep, and I sit here sobbing and wondering,

> asking God, "What purpose is there in this? Why did You take the love of my life? What do I do with the rest of my life? How will my heart ever heal?"

Shayla's Memories of Her Dad

My dad was a very warm, gentle, happy, funny, loving, caring, honest, respectable and godly man. To me and many others he was known as a big teddy bear.

My dad and I have been through some hard times but also some great times. One of the good times was when I was little. My dad used to give me whisker rubs. This occurred usually after four days of stubble was on his chin. It hurt real bad, but I would crawl back up on his lap for more. Shyanne got this treatment until Dad died. She crawled back up for more also. Another thing my dad was good at was snake bites. Even though it hurt I would go back for more. Funny how that works, eh?

My dad cooked the best sunny-side up eggs I have ever tasted. He really made the best cowpoke breakfast in the world.

As my mom homeschooled me I was given many opportunities to go with my dad when he worked for the forestry. He would go to different houses to give fire permits. That included coffee and conversation. The best treat was when he went to Gundy and I got to go. When we went to Dan Lefferson's house I would watch a movie and get a snack. Dad would visit and pray with Dan.

Dad got me my first pellet gun. He showed me how to shoot it and even set up a target for me. I hit it on my first try.

When Dad taught me how to drive the swather, he took me for two rounds, showing me what to do; then he let me drive it. He told me he would never drive with me in a car. He said a drunken man could drive a straighter line than me. But you know what? He was patient enough to stick with me until I got it right. When the swather would break down and Dad had to come fix it, I was amazed that those big hands could fix things so well. Those big hands were always rough from work, but whenever they touched you, you knew you were loved; you just felt it.

My dad's smile will always stay in my mind—in most people's, I reckon. When Dad smiled it would light up the room. My dad smiled all the time. He smiled right up to his dying day. Dad's smile was so big at my graduation. Uncle Dave said, "Well, she made it, George," and Dad said, "Yep, she sure did." And then there was that smile, and I knew he was proud of me.

My dad loved to joke and tease lots. Just before he got sick, I was leaving out the door and he hollered, "Shayla!"

I came back and asked him, "What?" He asked me how far I would have been if I hadn't come back. He teased lots with everyone in the family.

Number one thing for me about my dad, one I will never forget, is my daddy's big, beautiful voice. Oh how he could sing those hymns! In church Dad would sing bass. I would listen and close my eyes to feel it even more. When I would open my eyes and look up, Dad would be weeping as he sang praises to the Lord. It touched him that much. It was such an honor to see and hear my dad do that. Dad and I would sing and whistle together in church. He not only taught me to drive that swather but he also taught me to sing and whistle.

The last month of Daddy's life, as we sat and watched the Gaither videos, I told my dad that I would keep the old hymns alive. My dad would tap his feet and hands to the beat of the music right up to the time he died. He was always in beat. How cool was that?

My most precious memory, one that will always and forever stay with me, is simply this: As he lay in bed I crawled up beside him, and we of course were watching the Gaithers. Dad reached out and held my hand. When he did that I started to cry. I was so happy Dad did that, and then he reached up and kissed me on the forehead. We lay there for a couple of hours, just watching the Gaithers and holding hands. I was so happy that God gave me that special time with my dad.

I thank God for my family and for the special time for our family to say good-bye to Dad. God knew we needed that time. I thank God every day for giving us that chance.

Chapter Twelve

Lamentations 3:13

He pierced my heart with arrows from his quiver
(NIV).

I do not feel I knew one thing from the other after the diagnosis was presented to us. "Where is God in this?" I wondered. "How could He let this happen?" Was I ever going to survive without my precious country bumpkin by my side? Hadn't God heard my plea for our golden years to be without all the chaos? "Is this how You show Your love for us, God? Why would You want to do this to us? Didn't we always work towards the goal You set before us? Didn't You say You came to give us good things? Well, if this is all the good You've got for us, it plain old stinks. Where is there love in this?"

I remember nothing from the day of the memorial on December 23rd until Christmas morning. Many of the kids came for breakfast. Did I cook it? I do not know. I only remember them being there. I do not remember much else.

I do remember one day a dear friend, Caroline, came and crawled in bed with me when I thought I was going to die, or at least hoped to. I remember putting on George's Western jacket and taking his cowboy boots to hug. I was so mad at God. I remember telling Him I hated Him and that He was mean and nasty.

My daughter Shayla had told Caroline that I was out of control. In no time at all she was here. Many times those first few months Caroline was checking up on me and coming to the farm to spend time helping me.

My sister Ruby came to help me out as well. I needed this as there was one breakdown after another. Due to a water leak in the basement, the floor to ceiling had to be redone. The hot water tank went on the fritz. The washer and dryer did not work properly and had to be replaced. The dishwasher quit. The pressure tank and holding tank had to be replaced because of the leak. The waterline in the pond froze up, and it left me without water. My boiler boiled over. The wood ran low for the boiler.

My two oldest sons had to come repeatedly because of these breakdowns. Just before George died a friend, Dave Burake, came and rebuilt part of the basement floor and rerouted plumbing.

CHAPTER THIRTEEN

Lamentations 1:13

"He struck me with lightning, skewered me from head to foot. "

The name of this book, *Don't Tell Me It's Okay,* is to me a statement of impact. It is *not* okay, and it is not okay for people to tell you that.

There are a few things that should never—and I mean *never*—be said to a person who is grieving. One is that it is okay. Really? Tell me how it is okay to lose someone you love! People, think before you open your mouths! There are no great words of wisdom at a time like this.

The worst comment for me was the day after George died. This comment was "I have never seen you look more beautiful." I wanted to get up and punch the person right in the face. It took all the control I could muster not to do this. How foolish to tell someone who just lost the love of her life this! Put a bridle on your mouth at a time like this. It made me feel ten times worse. This is a cruel statement to someone who is grieving.

Another thing is, do not quote Scripture. If you are a Christian and have just suffered a loss you already know it. When the words do not match up with your feelings, you only feel more despair. There is too much anger and grief already, and this is the last thing a person wants at this time.

It may be true that some people do not feel angry at a time like this. I am not sure of this. I think some pretend because they do not want to appear to be ungodly. I know for me, due to my life in the past, I have learned to be bone-deep honest with myself. Some people get upset with me about this. When I can be honest with what I am feeling I can then deal with myself and my feelings and put them at the foot of the cross.

I am not going into all the dos and don'ts, for there are many good books on this. What I am going to say is, please, just be quiet. Cry when they cry; laugh when they laugh. Make sure they have a bite to eat. Clean up for them. Hold them, and phone them daily. Do not stop, not after a week or two, not even after a few months. Do not stop because you're too busy or you think they are okay. Set up a day and phone even if you're out of town or at someone's place. You do not need to have a big conversation with them if you honestly don't have the time. You just need to say, "I have called to pray with you. I can phone tomorrow, and we can chat, if that is okay." Pray and say good night. The person will appreciate this and understand that you have a life also. Leave a prayer on their machine if they are not there. They may be coming back from having to deal with some tough things, and prayer is always needed.

Your church should set it up so that there is one person an evening to call and pray with the grieving person. Do not let this go by the wayside. The pastor and board should be making sure that this is being done. This also should be for the first year. When it is a woman who has lost, the women need to phone and meet her needs; same for the men. The person in grief has a whole year of firsts. I truly feel people should be held accountable if they let this slip by or have a "reason" why they don't. This will happen in their family one day, and then they will find the need for it themselves.

When a church sets up a phone list but then does not use it even when it is asked for, it makes the grieving people feel like they do not count in the body of Christ. You can tell them they do, but if you don't show it, then you are a very shallow church. As I am a woman, it should have fallen on the women to keep this up. One sister in the Lord whom I dearly love was not even a member of our church. She phoned me constantly. She and her husband, precious people, took George's cows for us when he became ill. They sacrificed a lot to show their love. No amount of money can replace that kind of love and caring.

Don't just call and talk. Call and pray. I learned through my time of grief that when I could talk that was okay, but when someone prayed for me I had a better grip on myself.

I have been wounded by the church because of their lack of commitment. I feel that this church is not my church but my husband's church. I continue to go, but my heart is heavy with doing this a lot of the time. I do not know if I am to move on or not. Until I am able to again hear the voice of God I will stay put and work towards doing what I need to do to be an active member of the body of Christ.

I have been told that you will become an outcast within the church due to the fact you are now single. You will be a fifth wheel. I have talked to a number of single people regarding this, and they tell me that this nearly always happens. They also tell me that as a single person you will be cut out of lives when there are get-togethers. If you are in your mid-seventies, you are not a threat. You are getting to the age when you are not looking for a mate. I am not sure that this is true for me at this point, as I have not experienced this. Having a little one to raise also puts me in a different position. Maybe down the road when I am healed to some degree I may see that this is so. I pray not. At the present I do not even care if this is true or not. I am too deep in my pain to bother looking.

Chapter Fourteen

Lamentations 3:16

He has broken my teeth with gravel; he has trampled me in the dust (NIV) .

Outgoing E-Mail

I was asked to write a note about how I am getting along so the person can pray for me. I am not getting along.

I am reading a book called *Inside Grief* by Kathy O'Brien. I feel I wrote the book. Every person should read this book to understand even a fraction of the pain and misery that go hand in hand.

I know I have the signs of depression. I feel like the black hole I fell into is closing over top of me and I do not even want to try to get out, because when I even peek over the edge the pain is too great to handle. To even try to tend the fires is more than I want to do.

The only way I can function is to look at something and say, "Okay, maybe I can handle ten minutes to sweep the floor." I never seem to get to the point of putting it in the garbage, only swept to a corner or two or three piles around the room.

To take care of Shyanne is something I am only half doing. I am so consumed with tiredness that it seeps out of every pore of my being. I do not feel there is a hope and a promise for me.

I have to go to town to tend business. All I want to do is curl up and not exist. Each time I go to town I have loose bowels and I vomit. To be honest and humiliated, I also wet my pants one day, I was in such pain and torment. Then I have to go home and be a mom to Shyanne and pretend it is all okay.

People say, "Call me if you need something." I can't think straight, I don't care, and I don't know what I need. How do you make your needs known when there is nothing of you to do this? I am at the point I am too tired to try.

I spend hours on end just being empty. The pain I have over my heart since George's diagnosis has increased and I just don't care.

Incoming E-Mail

Sue,
Read your e-mail and I cried for you!

I pray and I cry for you but I cannot even begin to understand the pain and the loss you are feeling. Nor is there anything I can do at this point to lessen your pain.

The reason you feel you wrote the book (*Inside Grief*) is because you are not alone; others before you have felt their own loss, and there will be others following you.

Does this make it any better? No, I think not. I know others have survived the greatest loss (I believe), one's soul mate or kindred spirit. Sue, George would not want you to struggle as you are. He is rejoicing with the Lord. You would not want George to struggle if the roles were reversed.

All I think you can do at this point in time is take one minute at a time; then it will become one hour at a time; then, one day, one week, one month, one year. It does take time; do not put pressure on yourself to return to normal. Life will never be as it used to be. You will learn to cope in your own time. It is different for everyone, and there is no set time for when you feel stronger or even just able to make it through a day not totally consumed with pain, tiredness and grief. One step at a time, one day at a time.

You are a strong woman, Sue. You may not feel that right now, but you are. Each step you take forward is a result of your strength.

We will continue to pray for the emptiness to be filled with the wonderful memories that bring a smile and not a tear, for the pain to be replaced with acceptance and your tiredness to turn to a renewed strength for the future.

We love you and continue to pray for you. Remember, and let go and let God.

He will carry this heavy load you are struggling with. Give Him the chance.

Love,
John and Harlene

Incoming E-Mail

Bill is away and he forwarded me your message.

Thought I'd get up and wait for some great spiritual word before communicating to you. But no, I'm here and better that I share my heart through the tears that flow so easily when you communicate your heart than to wait for the sweet by-and-by that may never come.

Although I don't have any spiritual bandage that would make everything okay for you, and it's uncomfortable that I don't, I do feel very thankful and honored to hear your heart, because each time you share I become aware that this living can be nothing but "damn" hard. Then I hear you cry that He never leaves you or forsakes you, nor has He no matter how wrung out your heart becomes. So I pray strength for the moment, strength for the situation, strength for the day, yes, and strength for you, girl. So Sue I give the only thing I have and that is my intercession to hold you up before the throne of grace and mercy, knowing that He will bring you through and you will be given the strength to stand and wait upon Him. (Hope this message doesn't come across as religious; you deserve so much more.) As I think of your "gentle giant" a smile spreads across my heart and I'm thankful for knowing you both.

With much love and blessings towards you,
Diane

Shortly after George died I found my readings that I had prepared for my funeral when I die. Here is the letter I had written to George at that time:

To my darling husband,

Honey, you are the greatest gift that God has given me besides my salvation. If you are still here when I am gone, I anxiously await your arrival.

Don't hurry it though; enjoy this life God has given you.

Every time I try to think of what to say to you I cry. My love for you is so great. To leave you is the hardest thing that life has unfolded. I do not want you to mope for me or work yourself into exhaustion. Have special family time.

To you I leave our children. Look for me in them and our grandbabies. Enjoy them. See them for the gift they are. Share in their lives, and help them to see God's truths.

You have given to me more love than I ever dreamed was ever possible for another person to receive. The things I have in my heart I can't put on a page. I thank God for every last moment that I have had with you. I count it all joy.

Your loving wife

Incoming E-Mail

Sue,
I have no flowery words of great wisdom. All I have are words from my heart. I know what it is like to lose a mother, sister and best friend. I cannot imagine, Sue, what it is like to lose your soul mate. What I do know is that George would not want you to fall deeper into that hole of darkness. One minute, one hour, one day, Sue, the healing process will happen. You will one day find that the memories you and George made over the years will bring a smile to your face and perhaps a tear to your eye. You were fortunate to find such a great love with such a great man for all those years.

Please, Sue, don't let anything stop you from remembering those years with fondness and gratitude.

When the pain gets so bad, let go and let God, one baby step at a time.

I will pray for you to gain strength in this darkest time of your life. Know that we are here, Sue.

Love,
Mary Irene

Outgoing E-Mail

Please pray for me now. I can't quit crying. I am so empty, sad and tormented. Yesterday was a hard day for me, having to go do banking and groceries. This morning, just getting up, started with agonizing pain and tears. The day did not get better. I am tired of putting one foot in front of the other and pretending it is okay. I don't have the strength to keep pretending. My head hurts so badly. My heart hurts so badly, and I just can't do it today. I do not feel the Lord carrying me or even caring about me. How do I keep going? I just don't know or even care.

Incoming E-Mail

Dear Sue,

Thank you for your honesty. It is okay to feel these things. It's okay to not be able to pick yourself up. Just grieve. Allow your feelings to come so that healing can eventually come. I believe it will be slow, and you'll look back and think, wow, I've come a long way. It'll come. Just remember you are not alone. The Lord remains true and faithful and loving. Your feelings are real but not always truthful. Hang on to His promises, and know we all love you and are supporting you in prayer and however else you may need us.

Let us know. We love you, Sue.
Rhonda

CHAPTER FIFTEEN

Lamentations 2:13

***What can I say for you? With what can compare you, O Daughter of Jerusalem? To what can I liken you, that I may comfort you...? Your wound is as deep as the sea. Who can heal you?* (NIV) .**

Since my beloved has been gone, in less than three months one of George's brothers, an uncle and an aunt of mine have died. My grandson's best friend hanged himself. Shyanne has her ongoing medical problems. Also, the many other things mentioned in an e-mail.

Most days we go through George's stuff to get ready for the sale in June. With each piece of equipment being taken for sale a piece of George goes with it. So does my heart.

I shake and cry whenever I touch his stuff. I put my hands in his dress gloves and brush my arms with them. Oh, to feel his touch. I keep them in my dresser drawer, not able to separate myself from them.

My sister Dixie says you fake it till you make it. I think you fake it till you perfect the faking.

I find some people distance themselves from me as they do not know how to handle my grief. Neither do I.

I have lost many people that I have loved in my lifetime. But never someone I was in love with before.

I am that wounded animal the hunter shot, thought it was dead, skinned it out, only to have it jump up and run, bleeding profusely from its raw exposed meat.

The pain has made me feel crazy at times. I do not know what direction I am going in, I am so blinded by the pain. But I won't lie down and die, even though I so want to.

My joy is gone; my self-worth is gone. I was good at being his wife.

My sister Wendy tells me I have given so much to others over the years, far more than most people, and now is the time God wants me to give to myself. I do not know how to give to myself. I do not know what to do or how, and I am truly afraid.

Me! Being afraid is even hard for me to comprehend. After all the things I have gone through in life and I am afraid now. How is that possible?

When I look at myself I don't like what I see. I see a sniveling crybaby who is self-focused on my loss with an "I don't care" attitude.

I always had George, he was the rock of this family, and now I feel empty and so alone. The truth is, I may be lonely but never alone. I just don't feel God at this time.

I cry out to God to carry me through this, forgive me for my wrong attitudes and turn me into who He wants me to be. I feel abandoned by God as much as I feel abandoned by George.

I have tried to look deep within myself, and I was shocked at what I did see. *I loved George more than God.* I was trying to be the Proverbs 31 wife. My whole life was made up of trying to be a good mom and later nana. Mostly being that loving and giving wife. I put everything I had into this. I am so confused; was I so stubborn that I could not see this when George was alive? Is that why I had to lose him?

I feel that by the time June is finished—the ashes, my birthday, Father's day, the sale—I will not be able to crawl out of the pit. Joseph had a hand out of the well. Me, I do not think this will happen.

My children always thought they knew me. They find I am not that person they thought I was. I am not that strong mommy who will know what to do and make it okay. They are used to me being that pick-up-my-socks-and-get-going type of person. I feel they have been robbed of their mother. There is someone who looks like her but not someone who they know standing before them.

CHAPTER SIXTEEN

Lamentations 1:3
After affliction...she finds no resting place (NIV) .

My dear friend Shelley came to visit today, January 20th. George's birthday is today. It is our first time for his birthday without him.

I told her my struggles. Are they real or imaginary? Justified or not, they are still real for me.

I asked Shelley if she was able to tell me about her vision when George died. At the time she told me about it. She has since put it into story form for me. This is her vision and her thoughts regarding George:

> To the Grieving Heart
>
> There once was a godly mountain of a man named George. I was proud to call him my friend. Wherever he went he left behind hugs, laughter or a word from God. I believe he was a blessing to many yet remained a simple, humble farmer at heart.
>
> I remember I wanted to get close to him in church so I could enjoy his deep bass voice. That guy had a set of pipes on him and he was not afraid to use them.
>
> It is with a heavy heart that I write this, because my dear friend passed away in December of 2007. I wonder why we say *passed away* when in truth for some of us George was brutally torn from our presence.

Given a choice, some of us would plead, "Not George, please, not him." That was not to be. So we remain behind to grieve the loss of a great man whose parting leaves us with emptiness that only time and God can ever hope to fill.

Early one morning as I lay in bed, my thoughts and heart centered on the painful parting of my friend. Tears welled and poured down my face as I asked God, "Why George, God? Why him?"

I believe God in His infinite wisdom and mercy gave me a vision that I feel compelled to share.

Before me a large group was gathered. Excitement rippled through the crowd as they laughed and whispered to each other, looking towards a large entrance, waiting for something or someone. It was then that I heard the familiar beautiful bass voice belting out a song of praise. Yep, you guessed it. My friend had arrived in heaven.

Many family members and friends gathered around him to welcome him with hugs and to ask of loved ones left behind. George worked his way patiently through the crowd, sharing news of loved ones. Much rejoicing was heard, and some prayers went out for the unsaved.

On occasion I could hear George's laughter and I wondered if he was telling stories about us. We certainly gave him the ammo, and he could never resist a funny story.

It warmed my heart to see that even in heaven George was still doing what he always did, loving and encouraging people.

As he worked his way through the crowd he felt someone

tugging on his clothes. When he looked down he was thrilled to see his grandson Kyle and my son David. He scooped them up, giving them big bear hugs. He tickled them, gave them whisker rubs, and told them how much he loved and missed them. When he put them down, they raced away to play.

The crowd became still and quiet. George turned to see what had happened.

Before him stood Jesus, and George fell down and worshiped Him. Jesus touched his shoulder and told him to rise up. Jesus said, "Well done, my good and faithful servant."

Then Jesus said, "Speak. Tell me what is on your heart."

In a voice choked with tears, George spoke of his family. He asked Jesus to speak to the unsaved children and to draw them to Him. He asked for extra strength for his sons to endure in their faith, as they would face obstacles and difficulties. He knew his boys would be a strong support and comfort for their mother. He asked for much comfort and healing for his children.

"And for my wife Sue, I ask you pick her up and carry her. She will grieve the deepest and will need You so much. Please tell her that I love her and wait patiently to see and hold her again."

This is the vision that I saw. My hope is that you would receive a message of peace from it as I did. Love,
Shelley

Chapter seventeen

Lamentations 2:5
The Lord is like an enemy (NIV) .

Outgoing E-Mail

Today is three months to the day for George going home to the Lord. I have tried not to even know what this day is. If I didn't need to know the appointments for Shyanne I would not even look at a calendar.

They say it gets better in time. This I think is false; I think you learn to hide it better. You try to suck it up more, but inside you are in such pain that no one really sees the depth of it.

I am not sure, but it seems your spirit just knows the months and days. It seems the closer to the day your tears just want to flow and don't want to stop. The sad part about it is, I am so afraid to let it all go because I feel I will fall into a place I won't be able to come out of, or want to.

Today Shyanne got up and wanted her Western boots, shirt and hat for church. "Like Dad" she kept saying. She continues to want to go to Dad and Jesus.

I have asked people to pray that Shyanne will be still for

her CAT scan on the 18th. This is to see why her head is swelling and her legs are twisting and not working very well. Her migraines are increasing and so are her temper tantrums.

Shane and I are constantly going through George's stuff. Man, that guy could collect junk! Shane found things that he had thrown in the garbage at his place and George snatched up because they might come in handy some day. Pray for God to pour His blessings on Shane as he does this heavy task.

It is a good thing that Shane is more like me in that area. Now Ernie, on the other hand, wanted me to let him go through the throw-out stuff in case it might be good. Ring a bell to the person he is like in that way?

The auction sale of the equipment will be the 21st of June. I always wanted my yard cleaned up. Even though Shane is doing a bang-up job, it is also an empty feeling that comes with this.

I do not feel I have had time enough to take a breath and acknowledge that George is truly gone. I find I am looking at the door when I hear a sound, thinking he is coming in the house.

God says He comes to give me a hope and a promise; He comes to prosper me, not to harm me. Even though I do not feel this, I still cling to it.

I really need prayer to face each day as we deal with Shyanne. It is of no value to try to cut the tendons in her legs to straighten them when the brain is telling them to curl. It would be no good with the bones twisting in her legs as well. She can never have anything in her body, no shunts, no injections, no tubes, not anything. As to what to do, the doctor once said it was like throwing a needle in the ocean and then trying to retrieve it. Only God knows.

Thank you for your prayers and for the people that continue to come and see me and call. You have no idea what this means to me. May God truly bless you for doing these things!

I wrote this poem:

I sit alone night after night,
Wishing for my honey to hold me tight.
His big strong hands, so gentle and kind, I
can't get their feel out of my mind.
His lips always so warm and sweet.
The words "I love you, honey" he'd so often
say, Once or twice each and every day.
His smile so wide it would melt your heart,
Brown eyes that twinkled when his teasing hit the mark.
Lonely all day, lonely all night,
I long for my honey to hold me tight. I long to see that
big beautiful smile, Gentle teasing was his style.
I will continue to miss him as the years go by, One
day we'll be together in our home on high.

CHAPTER EIGHTEEN

Lamentations 1:1

Oh, oh, oh...How empty the city, once teeming with people. A widow, this city, once in the front rant of nations, once queen of the bal, she s now a drudge in the kitchen.

GOLDIE'S MEMORIES OF HER DAD

What to say about my dad? My dad was an honest, hardworking, big-hearted mountain of a teddy bear. He was a man of humility and integrity.

To say he wasn't born with a hidden horseshoe would be an understatement. He wasn't rich; nor did he ever win anything. He only recently started to travel some. He never got to redo that classic auto like he always wanted to do.

He loved a Cadillac, though he was never meant for one. He could live without all of that anyway. What he did have was even better than a Cadillac.

He had a wife, a friend, a love for forty years. He had numerous kids, theirs and everyone's. He had seventeen grandchildren and many Christian brothers and sisters who dearly loved him for the country gentleman that he was.

He was a lover of music. He had a beautiful baritone voice that will surely be missed in the church. God is truly enjoying it right now.

He took time to sing with us to teach us. I think this was more for him than us. He just could not stand a person murdering a song. I remember him listening to Jenny sing when she was in the kitchen. He was in the living room, and he made a comment that he had to spend more time with her.

My dad was a man who could instill the most basic feelings in me as a child. I have never felt safety like sitting on his lap as a small child. I remember dozing on his lap, feeling him breathe, hearing his heartbeat, listening to his voice sounding so far away. To a little girl nothing is more comforting than pretending to be asleep and Dad carrying you to bed.

On the other side of the coin, the words "Go tell your dad what you have done" can bring fear to any Doble child. I'll never forget as a child saying, "I'm sorry, Dad," and him saying, "You want to be." "I love you" were not words that rolled off my dad's tongue when we were little. When Dad found God, the words flowed freely without hesitation. He definitely became more attentive to his wife and kids after becoming a Christian.

The man who raised me and the man of today are two different people. I am honored to have known him as a father and a man of God. I know there have been a lot of regrets concerning us kids, but a more loving, caring father I could not find. My heart feels sorrow like I never felt before.

My family has experienced tragedy like we have never known. Only through God will we survive.

Chapter nineteen

Lamentations 3:19

I'll never forget the trouble, the utter lostness, the taste of ashes, the poison I've swallowed.

I was cleaning the bookshelves and found something I had written five years before:

> As I sat and pondered my life from the day that I met my husband, I wondered what I would pen. How could I ever begin to put down the words on paper that would truly describe our thirty-five years of marriage? Do I love him after all these years? Without a doubt my answer is yes.
>
> What is my definition of love, and does my love for him meet that definition? Yes, it does, and more. My idea of love has changed over the years and with that so have my feelings.
>
> When you are young the hormones have a major factor in a relationship. This so often becomes a feeling that love is based on. Because the act of sex is so often used to define love, people get confused and hurt. This happened to us as well when we were first married.
>
> I have also learned that there is a difference between the act of sex and honest-to-goodness making love.

So many people, I have found, never go deep enough in their relationship to experience this at a truly deep level.

I am so thankful that God is in my life, for He taught me what true love really is. Also, I learned the rewards from this.

As a person I cannot say I have always loved my husband as I could have or should have. I have been selfish, demanding and bitter at different times; for this I will always be saddened by my actions.

This is the man that God gave me, and I do love him with all that I can love. I have been asking God to work on me, to teach me more about love and applying this to my marriage.

One important thing I have learned is never look at your mate's shortcomings. Look at your own to change, and turn your mate over to the Lord. He is the miracle worker.

There is not a time when I think about him and how lucky I am to have this man in my life that I don't cry. To be without him would be like walking around without my skin, for I would be empty and wounded. I cannot even imagine what life would be without him.

I would lay down my life in a heartbeat for him. If I had the chance to care for him like a baby I would count it all joy as long as I could have him with me. I pray God allows me many more years to learn to love him as he deserves. For he has loved me far more than I have ever felt I deserved to be loved.

For this I am amazed and overwhelmed. I pray we have many more years.

Well, here we are five years after I wrote that, and wham! My beloved husband has departed from this life and is in paradise.

Was I kinder, more loving and more caring? Did I fill up my memory box with good memories? When the pain is under control more, will I have sweet memories? I'd like to think so. There is one thing I do know: we loved each other deeply. We were in love for most of our forty years. We did not just love one another or find ourselves comfortable. Being in love has a whole different meaning and feeling than loving someone. It is a rare and precious gift.

At the end of our marriage we had no unfinished business. This, too, was a gift of God.

I do have one regret, though. That regret is we did not have more time, those golden years that are so often talked about, when we could relax and enjoy the place God gave us. Forty years of marriage to me is just not enough time to have with this gentle giant of a man. I am not saying that we never had intense lack of fellowship. I am saying that at the end of the day, love ruled.

George and I were not always Christians. In fact, if God were not in our lives we would not be together today. When we accepted Jesus in our lives, personally and as a couple our lives turned for the better.

Where is my life going now? God is the only one who knows. I would not like to venture or guess, because at this time in my life I do not feel that God has any good thing for me.

I still have so much love inside of me that I daily gave to George. It hurts my heart not to have him here to give it to. I know that God should be the receiver of this love. Daily I am looking to trust Him, believe in Him, and most of all rid myself of the lie that God is punishing me. This is such a hard thing for me to do with the pain I feel each day. I have had so many people say, "Oh, Sue is so strong," but I have never been weaker, so confused or helpless and really, really frightened in my life before. I wonder why I use the word *I*. For I do not exist.

Chapter twenty

Lamentations 2:20
"Look at us, God. Think it over. Have you ever treated anyone like this?"

Outgoing E-Mail

Well, we are in our sixth month without George. His presence is ever so present. I was truly hoping that as time passed things would get easier.

With having to go through all of George's stuff I have gone backwards. It is other things besides. It is saying good-bye to a way of life, the business, all the machinery, tools, junk, and most of all my beloved. I miss him with every fiber of my being. It does not take just a few weeks to go through everything, but months.

I am so thankful to God for the help of the church body to get started on the valley. That is where George towed everything when the house yard got full and I started complaining my yard was looking like a reservation. There was an old house that was full of stuff from Rainier still. The helpers got a real insight to the collector that George really was.

Now that the junk and garbage is sorted out, the good

stuff has to be put on pallets and placed on the sale site on the farm. All the machinery needs to be moved to the sale site. Shane has a lot of the machinery already done.

I have worked for weeks going through the garage and around the yard, putting things on pallets. I would be safe saying I have fifty-plus pallets so far. I so often find myself sobbing over things, mostly tools that he has had for years and the memories that go with them. My thoughts so often wander to the times those big strong loving hands held those tools. The old metal stool we so often snuck back from one another because it fit the purpose for both of us. The set of tools from his dad he had since he was fifteen that he treasured so much. The number of hoses or extension cords he kept because there was a good end on them or maybe a clamp. How about all the cans of paint he took out of Shane's trash, thinking they still might be good, and still having them eight years later, having been frozen all winter that many years? The list goes on and on about his collected stuff.

I have found myself angry at God and giving Him the gears. This was George's mess; why do I get the privilege of cleaning it up? Why is Shyanne without a daddy? Why at sixty am I alone to raise a challenged kid? My ranting at God goes on and on till I fall on my face and seek forgiveness; then I start all over again the next day.

I have dreaded the thought of June coming. On Father's Day, the 15th, we are spreading George's ashes on the farm. Each of us has our own memory spot of Dad. We will each take some of his ashes and say our final good-byes. Then the 16th will be the sixth-month day; seems like yesterday. The 18th will be my 60th. Don't want to think about that one. Then the 21st will be the sale of his life's collection. I know that he is not dead, that only his body is. George is ever present with the Lord. It just does not take the ache away. I am blessed that we shared a deep love. Not everyone gets to have that, and I was blessed with forty years. We had many times of intense lack of fellowship, but our love was stronger than the problems.

I am booking a flight to Newfoundland for ten days after the sale. This too will be a first, as George and I traveled together and this was to be our trip in May. I am praying I can come back and be able to face the rest of my life without him.

I have always wanted the yard cleaned up, but this was not what I was thinking at all.

God says He has a hope and a promise for me. It just makes me afraid right now, and I know I should look at it as an adventure. I am going to go to Bible school in the fall if things go as planned, and I am starting to write again.

The nights are hard, as I do not get much company. Please pray that I get through this month. I know that I have sunk back into depression over doing this stuff. I do not let many people into my life in case they really see me. People don't know what to do with hurting people, so they shy away as a rule.

Even my letterhead has to be changed. This too is a memory that must go.

My oldest daughter and I are estranged, and that saddens me. It would have broken George's heart and made him angry at the way I am being treated at this time. It has hurt me more than she will ever know or care to know. This should not be. It has not helped at all with the healing to have this happen. It is sad when a person cannot put wanting their own way aside for even a little while. Please pray that she would soften her heart and look at herself and make things right.

Thank you for your prayers and support.

As I write this it is not to single out anyone; it is to help people understand. If you care even one little bit about someone, please, please, give him or her space to grieve. If you do not do this, you have no idea of the scars you are adding to the person's already wounded heart. It is a far greater hurt than even I could ever imagine it would be, not just to me but to the rest of the family, who saw me go through this added pain.

There were a few times when I really contemplated suicide, not just my life but Shyanne's as well so she wouldn't be without a mom. I went to a counselor, so I did not do this. I felt I could not make it without George, and I also felt that the kids would have preferred that I went instead of George. I have felt that my oldest continues to punish me because it was not me. I truly wish it had been me. What a wonderful place to go to. No private island could compare to there.

What I have felt in my despair is not necessarily the truth. It is something I am continuing to work on as I heal. As my teacher says, unpack it till the truth of the lies emerges.

If you are grieving also over the loss of a loved one, then you are not thinking with a clear head either and need to back off so there can be healing, instead of stealing the healing.

The best way I can describe the pain I have from not letting us have a chance to heal is this: I feel like I had radical surgery on my heart. This was done by a very incompetent surgeon. The heart now has a very deep crevice with many unnecessary ugly deep-red scars.

As God's anointing oil has been poured out on my heart, the scars are turning from an ugly red to a soft pink. One day they will be flesh-colored. The thing is, the scars and the cavity from the ripping and tearing of the heart will always be visible; they just won't hurt at the end of the healing. Praise God for His healing power!

People, please let the past hurts go. You accomplish nothing but add more pain when you try to prove you are right or you feel slighted, hurt, angry or any other thing that gets in the way of healing and being a family. If you can't let it go, you will destroy the people you say you care about and destroy yourself in the end. People, please hear me: it isn't worth it at the end of it all. Everyone suffers.

Remember that life is but a breath away from death. Your energy should be used for caring and loving.

As Christians we are told to forgive people who offend us seventy times seven times (Matthew 18:22). It takes a lifetime to build relationships and a moment to tear them apart.

CHAPTER TWENTY-ONE

Lamentations 5:20

"So why do you keep forgetting us? Why dump us and leave us like this?"

When I think I can handle some tasks around the house I find that there may be heartache lurking in the corners. I found years of cards George had saved that I had given him. What I found behind the bench on George's side of the bed both broke my heart and gave me peace all in one breath.

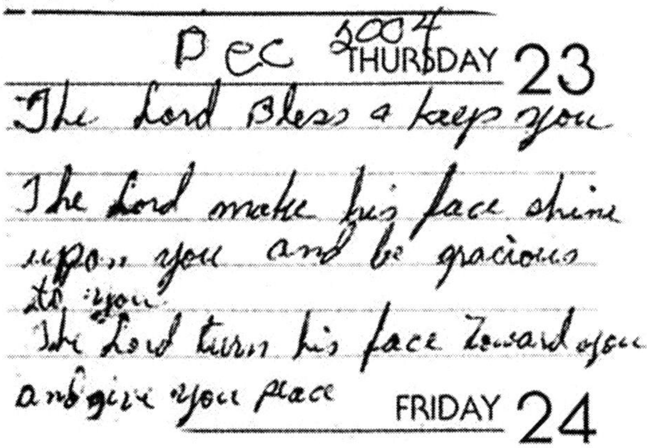
Dec 2004 THURSDAY 23
The Lord Bless & keep you
The Lord make his face shine
upon you and be gracious
to you
The Lord turn his face toward you
and give you peace FRIDAY 24

I found a datebook of his for 2004 in his portfolio. I usually throw them out at end of the year. How did I miss this one? God knew I would need it in my darkest hours. George never wrote Scripture down. He always said it was a waste of paper—it is already written down in the Bible.

This was written three years to the month before George's death. How cool is that? Only God could do that. God also knew I would have to see it in George's handwriting to have it sink into my heart.

It is Father's Day, the day to spread George's ashes. For six months they have sat on my bathroom shelving unit. I have talked to him, cried to him, swore at him, and told him that when I get to heaven I am going straight up to him and kick him in the butt for leaving me and for the heartache I have been going through without him to rely on. I have talked over the things I usually talk to him about. I also have asked him, "How come you get to go and I have to stay?"

Now I have to take his ashes out of the urn and divide them up, and each of us will say our good-byes. Why? To try to have some form of closure. The hurt I feel trying to do this does not feel like closure but agony.

All of my children except Brendon came for the ash spreading. Some of our grandchildren and the brother of George's heart, Dave, and his beautiful and loving wife, Rose, were also present. I had bought flowers, memory flowers I called them. Daises were for the grandchildren, roses for the rest of us. Each person told a memory of George.

I wish I could remember them all, for each one was precious to me. I found myself in such agony and hyperventilating. I thought that I was going to pass out from the emotional pain, and the pain over my heart was so great. I do not remember what order things were done in or who spoke. I do remember Gordon telling how George would say, "How many eggs, Gord?" And I remember that the memory I shared was one that for forty years I have held dear.

My most precious memory was when early in our marriage I was overwhelmed with how much love George showered on me. I asked him, "Honey, how can you love someone like me so much?"

He started naming off the reasons. "You're gorgeous, you're funny, you're so loving and smart. I love your temper; you're sexy and hot, and a good cook, too. Most of all, you love me." I will always carry this close to my heart as if it were carved into it, never to be erased.

I brought my share of the ashes home to put on the pansy bed. These were George's favorite flower. When I got home I went to the garage to get the stool we each claimed, and I sat by his pansies and sifted his ashes through my fingers. My thoughts were all over the place, but my mind kept coming back to the fact that I would never hold him or caress him with my fingers in any form ever again. My whole life has been anything but easy. I should be tough enough by now to go through this with smooth sailing. Why is this still so raw and painful for me?

I feel like the agitator of a washing machine whipping back and forth, trying to get the stain out. For me the stain is the pain. Is God going to put me in the dryer also? If I go in before the stains are gone, will they be set in for good? I pray not.

Why did God deny my plea for a future with my beloved? Why was my mountain cast away from me? Why does something like this draw most people together and turn some against you?

I have no answers. I have only pain. I have questions upon questions that I would like answered, but God does not speak to me. Even this I question. Has He abandoned me as well? Or maybe I really am important to Him and He is holding, rocking and soothing me at the times I want to cash it all in.

I question my life as a wife. Whatever my husband wanted to do, I put my hand to the plow and made his dream my dream. His friends became my friends and mine went by the wayside when we were first married. His interests became my interests. I did all this to be a good wife. Later in life as I met the Proverbs 31 wife in Scripture I was even more determined to do this.

Are we not told in Scripture that God needs to be first in our lives? Have I dishonored God by putting so much emphasis on my mate? Is that being a good daughter of God's?

If you put your heart and soul into your marriage and it has ended, what is left of you? You are no longer your husband's wife but only you. Who are you? With this said, where is your starting place to become you and not someone's shadow?

Shane and I are cleaning out the fifth wheel trailer to get it ready to sell. Another dream gone, another memory to face. I tell Shane when I get to heaven I am going straight up to his dad and kick him in the butt for leaving me and me having to do this. Shane tells me to tell Dad he's going to do the same when he gets there.

I find our travel envelope with all the places and maps. I am crying hard now, and I see a verse number written on the back of the envelope. I say, "God, what are you trying to tell me through George now?" I go into the house and look it up in the Bible. Numbers 6:24-26, the same verse George wrote in his datebook: "*The LORD bless you and keep you; the LORD make his face shine upon you and be gracious to you; the LORD turn his face toward you and give you peace*" (Numbers 6:24-26, NIV). I pray for this Scripture to be a part of my daily life. Lord, how I need this now till my going Home.

CHAPTER TWENTY-TWO

Lamentations 3:6

He locked me up in deep darkness, like a corpse nailed inside a coffin.

It is ten months since George left us. This is the month of our wedding anniversary. I am in school and working at home to get things done up for the winter.

God bless Shane and Terry. How would I ever get through this without them? George always did things in bits and pieces, very seldom completing one thing. Shane is trying to get things done so I can handle them on my own.

May many blessings unfold for Pastor Roger and his sons for taking on the task of cutting my winter supply of wood for heating our house. I am humbled and thankful for their caring towards me.

God told me to give up all my hopes, dreams, wants, and all else. He has asked me to just praise Him. I try to do this but do not seem to keep at this like I need to.

I am not sure if I will stay here or move. I am torn when I think about it. I have to turn it over or I will sink back to that hole. There the suicide thoughts come. I cannot go there again.

Tomorrow is Canadian Thanksgiving. So, God, as today is a sad day, I choose to give thanks to You for my family.

We are doing things differently this year and having some young people in who are not around family at this time. Some of my children will come, some not. Family dynamics are different, but I do have family that love and care for me.

I am more than thankful for the weather. This has made it so much easier to handle, as I can be outside most of the time.

I am working to make the place mine, things I always wanted to have done. Someone said to me if George drove in the yard he'd probably drive back out thinking he got the wrong place. It is a wonder what cleaning up the junk will do. I truly love my place; I just need to learn to love the quiet and spend that time with God.

I do find I am still angry at George. It seems like a safe place to be, as the tears do not fall as fast. I want to laugh and find joy again. Sometimes I think I see a crack open and see the sun shining in my heart once again. Never in my wildest dreams did I ever imagine I would feel such pain. I too thought I was tough.

Again God is extracting more from me. This I fight like hell when it happens. I tell God, "Build me up from my grave's ashes and do what You want with my life." Then when He does I start in to fighting with Him. I holler at Him, "Haven't you taken enough from me? What's up with this? Where is there any reason behind what You are asking of me now?"

What is He asking? I don't want to acknowledge it, so He has turned up the heat on me. He wants me to give up Shyanne.

As I sit here and write this the tears fall from my face and the ever-constant pain over my heart since George died increases. I am so tired, worn and weary. It seems these feelings soak my clothes like perspiration on a hot summer day.

God says to give Him everything. But He won't take my life and lead me home to the Promise Land.

My friend Shelley and I talked at length today about how we have been survivors. We want to be more than survivors, because God says there is more to life than that. Why do we as humans so often look at the next season in our lives with fear and trepidation? Why do we forget to praise God for the blessings of the day and whine about what we don't have? Why do we put self on the throne and knock God off of it?

Oh, for the sin nature. I know I am tired of it in me. So as God asks me to give over Shyanne's care to Him I will praise our mighty God for the goodness of allowing me the privilege of being His servant in the care and love I have given her, for she has given me far more back.

He may not remove her from my home; it is the surrender that He wants. Let go of my desires for anything that will hold me back from being what God wants me to be.

Tomorrow would have been our anniversary. I am choosing to be thankful to God for the time spent with George. I cannot go back and change anything, so I choose to go ahead and get excited about my life by seeking the Father's will for my life.

Whatever plans God has for my life, I pray that I do not get ahead of Him but hold His hand and go where He directs me. I know now for sure that God has always held my hand. Sometimes He walks on the sandy shore and I in the billowing waves of life's ocean; sometimes He lets me walk on the shore with Him. He does this so I will trust in His holding on to me no matter what.

Chapter Twenty-Three

Lamentations 5:19

And yet, God, you're sovereign still, your throne intact and eternal.

October 28th would have been our anniversary. I purposed in my heart to live in grace, to not continue to be mad at George but to remember our wedding day in love and laughter.

The laughter is because of our wedding night. Our best man was to have booked our motel room in Brooks. We had been married in High River and had our reception in Okotoks.

Well, to continue with the story, we hit the hotel about 4 in the morning; the door to our room was to be open. The only thing was, we did not know the room number. George went into three different rooms that were unlocked, only to find someone in each of the beds.

We talked it over and decided we would go get our bed (box spring and mattress) from George's grandpa's farm. Then we would continue on to the house we had bought in Scandia. We hit the farm around 5:00 a.m. We found the box spring in the bathtub. Then we found our mattress in the attic. We hauled these out to the car and put them on the roof. Then we took off to our first night in our home. We got halfway to our destination and discovered we had lost our bed.

Now we really had a problem. George, being the sweet man that he was, had wanted me to have a nice ride on our wedding day, so he had traded his truck for a car for the occasion. Problem was, the car did not go in reverse. We then had to go around the country block, approximately eight miles, to pick up our bed.

There we were, with the box spring on the roof, with us holding it on, and the mattress on the hood. We nearly froze our hands off, but we made it to our house. George had to put the bed frame together and bring in the box spring and mattress while I looked through boxes for sheets, blankets and pillows. By the time we got this all taken care of we were hungry and really wanted coffee. We took off for his parents' house.

And so our marriage began. The next forty years were in many ways as eventful as our wedding night. You know what? I miss all that now, but I am so thankful that God gave us that time.

Grief is really messy. I do know one thing for sure, and that is without God I would not have made it. I have lost before and had great sorrow, but never like this. I guess that is something that we need to think on as people. You do not ever know the depth of another person's pain. Please be gentle and patient with one another. I must confess that I have not always been this at this time in my life. I felt I was fighting for my life and people were trying to destroy me. It may not be true, but in my grief that is what I felt.

Through my pain I have missed others' pain. I feel bad about this, but it is the truth.

In the Scriptures, Paul talks about how loss and death are a part of life (1 Thessalonians 4:13-18). Believers in Jesus can face them, as we are only saying, "See you later, honey; have a wonderful time in heaven."

I can hardly wait till I get to go Home too and see the face of God and see that big beautiful smile as I enter heaven's gates. I will get to see so many relatives and hold my husband, my first grandchild, my foster baby, my sister, George's parents, my dad and so many others. Because Christ lives, death is not a tragedy but triumph for those He loves.

Another thing I have learned is that God never punishes us. Christ came to set us free from the punishment of sin. I knew this mentally but not emotionally. What God does though is put us through very grueling discipline for the marathon of hope that to me is His kingdom's work.

George's kingdom work is not finished, even after death. It is through his death and his faith that reached out to so many that there are a number of people who have really sought out God. Before and after George's death this has happened.

I also pray that I can be faithful through this discipline as I am going towards a goal: that God's glory will shine through me.

Does all this mean I am done grieving or don't miss George? Not by a long shot. There are days that this happens in mounting waves. Whenever any of these days or moments come, I crash and cry and moan and weep. Sometimes this is for a few minutes, sometimes a few hours, and yes, sometimes for a few days.

Today is a "Honey, I miss you" day. In the midst of it as I am crying and the waves of loneliness wash over me, I cry out to God, "You are worthy to be praised. You are the restorer of my soul."

CHAPTER TWENTY-FOUR

Lamentations 5:1

"Remember; God, all we've been through. Study our plight."

We are now into the eleventh month. It is snowing, and with the cold comes cold feelings over my heart.

"We should have been in Florida right now" is my thought. Instead, I am at my computer writing out my heart on pages. This at times frightens me. I do not like to have people see the raw me. Why do I do it then? I feel compelled to do this. I believe with my whole being God wants this of me.

I am starting to see a bit of light into what He is calling me to do for Him. I am working out a program for the churches to step up to bat and help those who are hurting in the ways that I believe God wants us to. This will be as new for me as it is to other believers, but it is something I must do.

I am going on a date with my oldest son tonight. I am trying to do the things I would want George to do if he were the one left, having quality time with my children and grandchildren. Some I cannot do this with, as they have been removed from me. So I thank God for what I do have and will try to do my best with them. I pray for restoration for my family.

This is the 10th of November. I took George's chair apart to reupholster it. There were springs gone and wood that was breaking as I took it apart. I have made the choice to throw it out. I could fix it, but I choose to keep the memories. Memories are a wonderful thing if we choose them to be. I choose them to be. The chair is just an object.

Lots of necking went on in that chair. See, it is the memories that are important, not the chair.

I have painted the front room. I did it in greens, not because that is my color but because I think green sure is God's, with all the green He has in the world.

I finished my great-grandma's couch and chair and also the beam that George had been going to get done for so many years I can't remember.

The hardest thing I did this week was to put George's name in the record of death in our family Bible. Even as I write this I cry. I shook, and a couple of times I thought I couldn't do it and closed the book.

Then I remembered "*I can do all things through Christ who strengthens me*" (Philippians 4:13, NKJV). It is just so final. There is no denial, no turning back from this point on. I need to let go of all the things that cause me pain and do what God would have me do.

It is Sunday, November 16th, and I am going to church. This is the day a year ago that when I awoke I found my husband had a fractured mind. One month to the day from that point in time till he went home.

Today I sat and was thinking, *If someone finds out who I am, I sure hope they let me know also.*

In school we were to do our thought analysis for a week. I got three days done and quit. I realized I have been functioning without thinking for the last year. Doing the thought analysis showed me what a robot state I was in and how I could not get past the pain until I learned how to think along with the function part. I did not like this. I thought I was in a safe place, and it was a lie. It was a painful, ugly place. Now I know the truth, I have to change this.

Yesterday was the 20th of November, the day a year ago we were told the news. I chose to have a good day. My son Ernie's wife, Kim, gave Ernie a bang-up birthday party at his shop. I did not go but was so happy for this. I am glad for new beginnings for him. He has had a number of hard things happen on his birth date, not just with his dad. Way to go, Kim!

As I look back over the last four years, I see the handiwork of God. He was helping me to prepare for a life without George, one that is not full of a pile of regrets.

God gave us a chance to travel, even if it was only a few times. God gave us countless trips to town together, shopping for groceries, where we laughed, talked, held hands and flirted with each other. God led us to make up our wills a year ago. God blessed George with financial stability and helped George have confidence in himself with this. God blessed George with the truck he loved, his boat and the tractor.

God also brought about deep healing in our marriage and freed us of past pains. God gave me the strength to care and love my husband at home till he went to heaven.

God removed some people from my life, even for a season. This I believe was so I would not be codependent and give my control away except to God.

God gave me a desire to write again, and I wrote various short stories over the last four years. God gave me the opportunity to go to Bible school, where I have learned more than I can believe. I learned to deal with the inner me. Thank you to Sharon; God's blessings on you and your teaching.

God has showered me with family and friends that love me apart from George.

Most of all, God showed me that He loves me, and accepts me right where I am at. God will supply all my needs (Philippians 4:19). I can trust Him.

God has a mission for me, and I thank Him that He cares for me so much that every detail for my life has been worked out. Even though I did not see it and do not have the whole picture, I can trust Him with my life. God is good and just.

I am reminded in Philippians 4:6-7, *"Don't fret or worry. Instead of worrying, pray. Let petitions and praises shape your worries into prayers, letting God know your concerns. Before you know it, a sense of God's wholeness, everything coming together for good, will come and settle you down."* Isn't that awesome? Is that not the way we are to live? We cannot do this without knowing the Lord as our personal Savior. Do not delay! Take the time now and ask Him into your heart and give Him your life to do His will in you and through you.

Chapter Twenty-Five

Lamentations 3:55,56

"I called out your name, O God, called from the bottom of the pit. You listened when I called out. 'Don't shut your ears! Get me out of here! Save me!'You came close when I called out. You said, 'It's going to be all right.'"

November 23rd became a day of "Will I really surrender to the will of God or do my own thing?" I talked with my friend only to discover that God wanted more from me than I felt I could give. I mentioned to Shelley, "I hope God never asks me to take George's picture or his wedding ring off from around my neck."

Shelley's statement to me was something like this: "I think you already know what God wants or you would not have thought of it." I started to cry. Shelley then asked me, "What about if you just take it off at night?" I cry more and say I cannot do this. Why? George had been my protector for those forty years. We had slept in our bed together for all these years. I am shocked at my feelings and cling to the chains on my neck. After getting off the phone I ask God to please just let me have them at least till the new year. I do not sleep all night.

I go to school the next day, and Sharon talks about idols in our lives, things that hold us back from God. I am shaken and I say, "But God, George was my protector." God speaks to me and says, "I am your husband; I am your protector."

I start to cry and have to leave the classroom. If these things around my neck were not idols they would not affect me like this. I still do not take them off. "Please, God, wait till tomorrow!" How do I give them up? I even think that if I buy longer chains and put them around my waist it will be okay. I know the truth; I just don't want to face it. The spirit of rebellion runs strong in me. I tell God, "Tomorrow." I do not sleep, and I cry all night.

The following day my friends and I meet for Bible study. I am a mess emotionally. We have prayer, and then I have Shelley take them from my neck. I know that all there is and all I need is God. Why the rebellion and the fear? This is the final chapter and close of a life I have led.

I am not fully trusting God. How do I feel about the process I have just gone through? Drained, emotionally and physically, and plain-old worn out.

I know I would not have gotten to this emotional state if I had not have been rebellious, if I had trusted God for all my needs. For this I repent and know that God's love and grace abounds. I wonder how people do it without Jesus.

Mark 16:17 says, "*They will speak in new tongues*" (NIV). God has revealed to me today that my new tongue is to be one of continuous praise rather than one that speaks despair. No matter how difficult it may seem to me, I must trust God to work out every detail of my life. I must move upwards on the ladder of praise.

Isaiah 53:3-4 simply tells me that He has left me without human support so that I would turn totally to Him. God will validate my life in the clear light of day and stamp me with approval at high noon (Psalm 37:6).

This is from God, all that I have gone through, that at the end of it all God would be glorified. I will not pretend to understand it, nor do I have to like it, but I must obey.

The prayer of praise is the highest form of communion with God as far as I am concerned. We do not do it because we feel good; rather, it is an act of obedience. When we do this even when our will does not want to, we give God the room to work in our lives in ways we never felt possible. But we should never do it to get something from God but because He is worthy of this very thing.

When I feel I will fall and crash, God tells me each time that He comes to prosper me and not to harm me; He comes to give me a hope and a future (Jeremiah 29:11).

God has assured me that it is okay for me to cry. This is not a sign of weakness but of someone who knows how to love deeply. I am not a weak person but one who has loved with all that I have. The hardest thing I am still going through is giving up being in love with George. I am learning to love the memories and give the love I had for George over to God.

As I walk with my Lord my prayer is that those who follow my footprints will be led to Christ.

I found the strength to make memory quilts for my children out of their dad's clothes. This too is a chapter closed. The quilt patches are made from both George's work jeans and good jeans. The edges are strips from his favorite shirts. On the back of each quilt I put a back pocket from the jeans and filled them with pictures of their dad. They can now cuddle with him in their own way and hold their memories in the pockets of their hearts.

It has now been a year without my beautiful country bumpkin. Tomorrow being December 16th, we will celebrate the life we were blessed to have with George. I choose to close the pages before that day and keep the memories in my heart's treasure chest. Praise God for His strength. His mercies are new every morning (Psalm 55-57).

God, You did everything You promised, and I'm thanking You with all my heart. You pulled me from the brink of death, my feet from the cliff-edge of doom. Now I stroll at leisure with God in the sunlit fields of life.

Epilougue

It is coming to the third year. Where has my life gone since then? It has begun in a different way. The families have been torn apart from not dealing with grief, blame, attack and defend.

I have moved to a new place with Shyanne, trusting God for new beginnings. I learned that with all the mess that I was in emotionally and physically that I never really grieved George. I grieved the things, but not him.

I fill my life now trying to take care of Shyanne and her needs, also reaching out to the seniors. Shyanne in herself is a full time job with her high needs. This is not easy at my age. I struggle with tears each and every time she hears a rich deep baritone voice on the radio or C.D. She runs to it hollering, dad, dad. She thinks George is singing to her from heaven. It gives her comfort and brings me pain. Maybe one day I to will have that comfort.

Time sometimes needs time. That is what the family needs to hopefully deal with their anger, and pain. Our family has fallen short of asking questions to make sure we understand one another instead of assuming; which causes more hurt. We all have changes and forgiveness to come into our lives so we can be better people. Most importantly we need God in a deeper way.

Sue Doble was married to George for forty years before the Lord took him home. Sue has had many hardships in her life. A challenging child hood turned into many challenges in her married life. Sue is a mother of 3 biological children, three adopted and another who became a child of the heart but not adopted. Fifty four foster children came through the doors of her home. At present there are seventeen grand children. Each child is a delight in their own way. Sue has and continues to raise a challenged granddaughter for ten years.

Hard times have always been a part of everyday life for her family. Sue watched her first grandchild be born dead. There has been grief and loses in many forms in the family's life.

What she has learned over the loss of the love of her life for forty years is that we as people each grieve in different depths over different people or different circumstances.

There is a form of grief that appears to rip the very soul out of a person and loosing George was that for her.

This book comes from her retching pain and all the love that came at this horrible time in her life. It is about the love of God holding you tight when you feel you are forsaken.

CPSIA information can be obtained at www.ICGtesting.com
Printed in the USA
LVOW071855181011

251066LV00001B/30/P

9 781452 087849